Artwork and text by Peggy Louise Parrish
Peggy Louise Parrish
Parma, Idaho 83660

Printed in The United States of America
ISBN-13:978-1544828657

The Zealous Letter Z

Coloring Book

By Peggy Louise Parrish

C. 2017

You have now come on an adventure with the Letter Z. You may color the Black and White designs of Z in this book any way you would like. There are several examples to inspire you. The most favorite coloring choice for these pages is a high quality colored pencil set. Some people prefer markers, gel pens, watercolor pencils or paints to color with. If you choose these place a piece of paper behind your page while you are working.

This is just part of a whole series of Letter Wonders. If you enjoy this letter try another letter book. One artist, Peggy Louise Parrish has originated the letter designs in the whole series. She has had fun coloring them, printing them out on different paper and even adding embellishments for cards or gifts. If you want to make a few in house copies of these letters to color and print out in different ways you may. She asks that you not sell anything made from this book. and leave the initials PLP on the bottom of the letter. Have plenty of fun with it!

Welcome to just a small part of the Letter Z World!

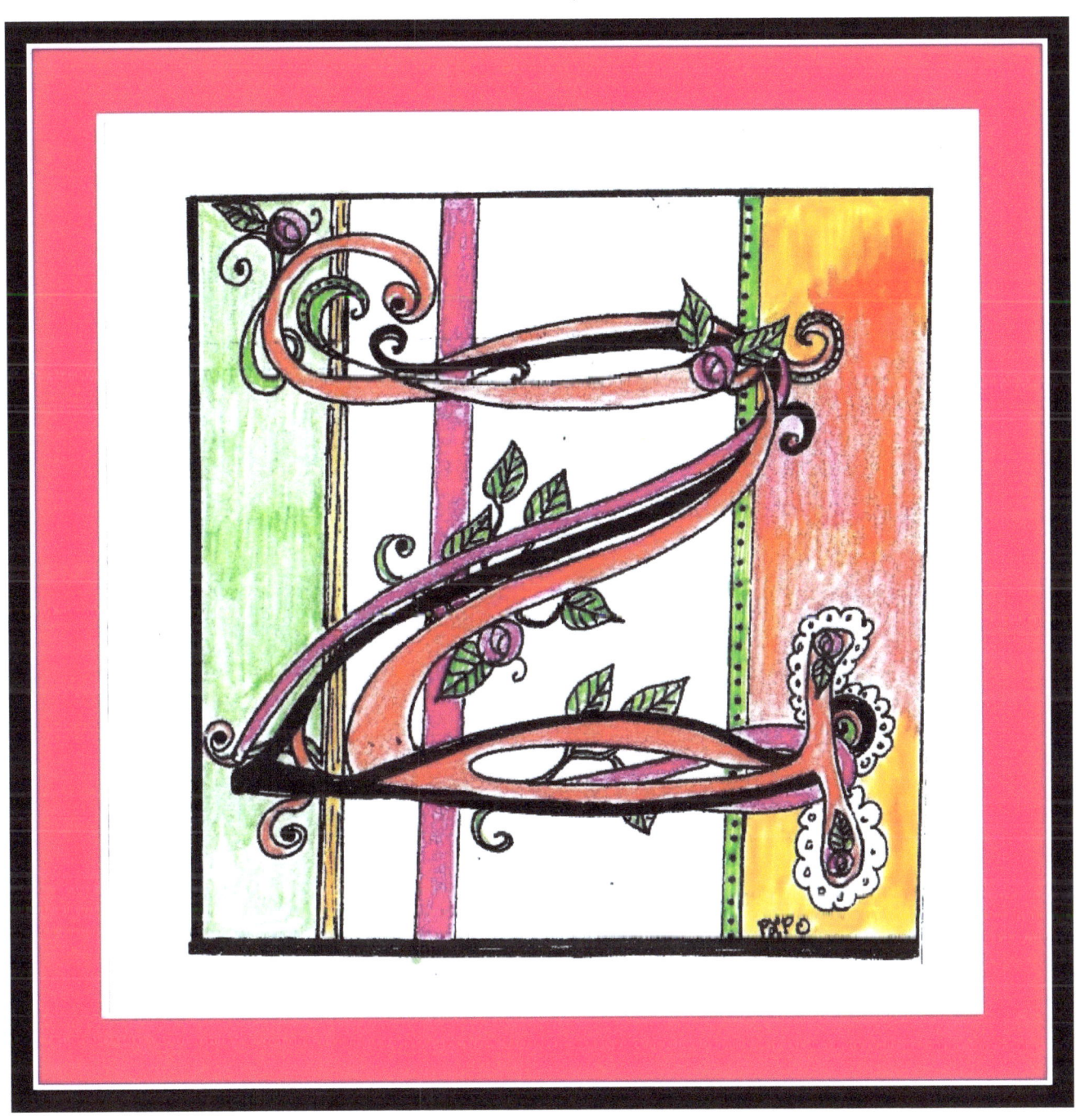

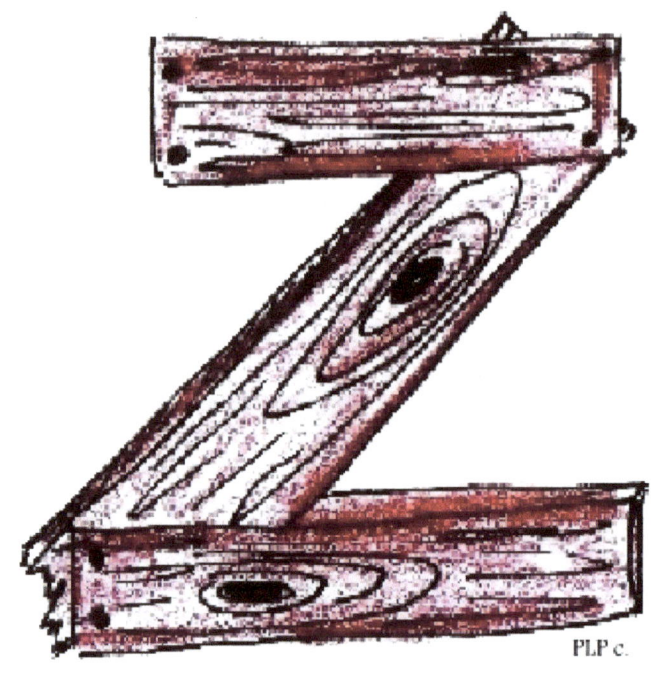

Color some Zs any color you want. Try a cowboy Z made out of lumber.

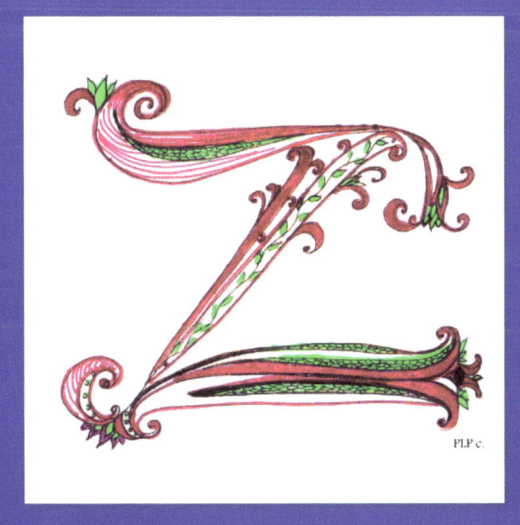
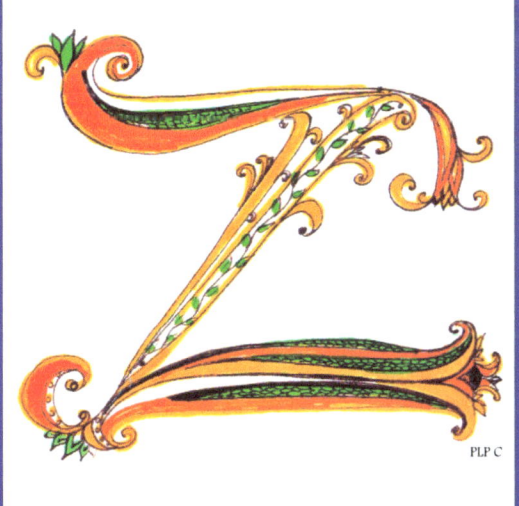
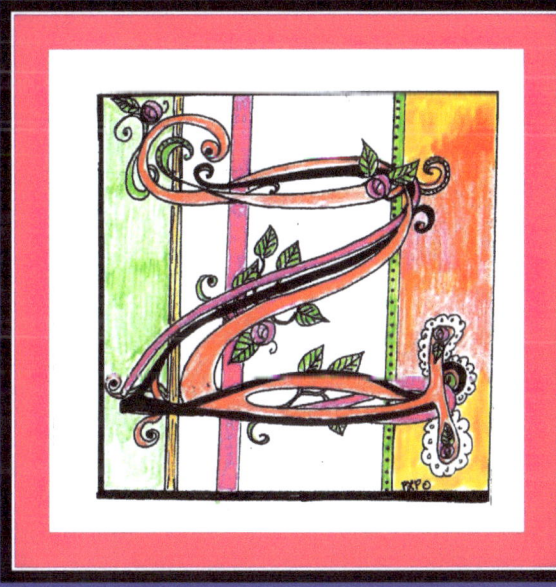

Letter Z is not boring to draw and color

9

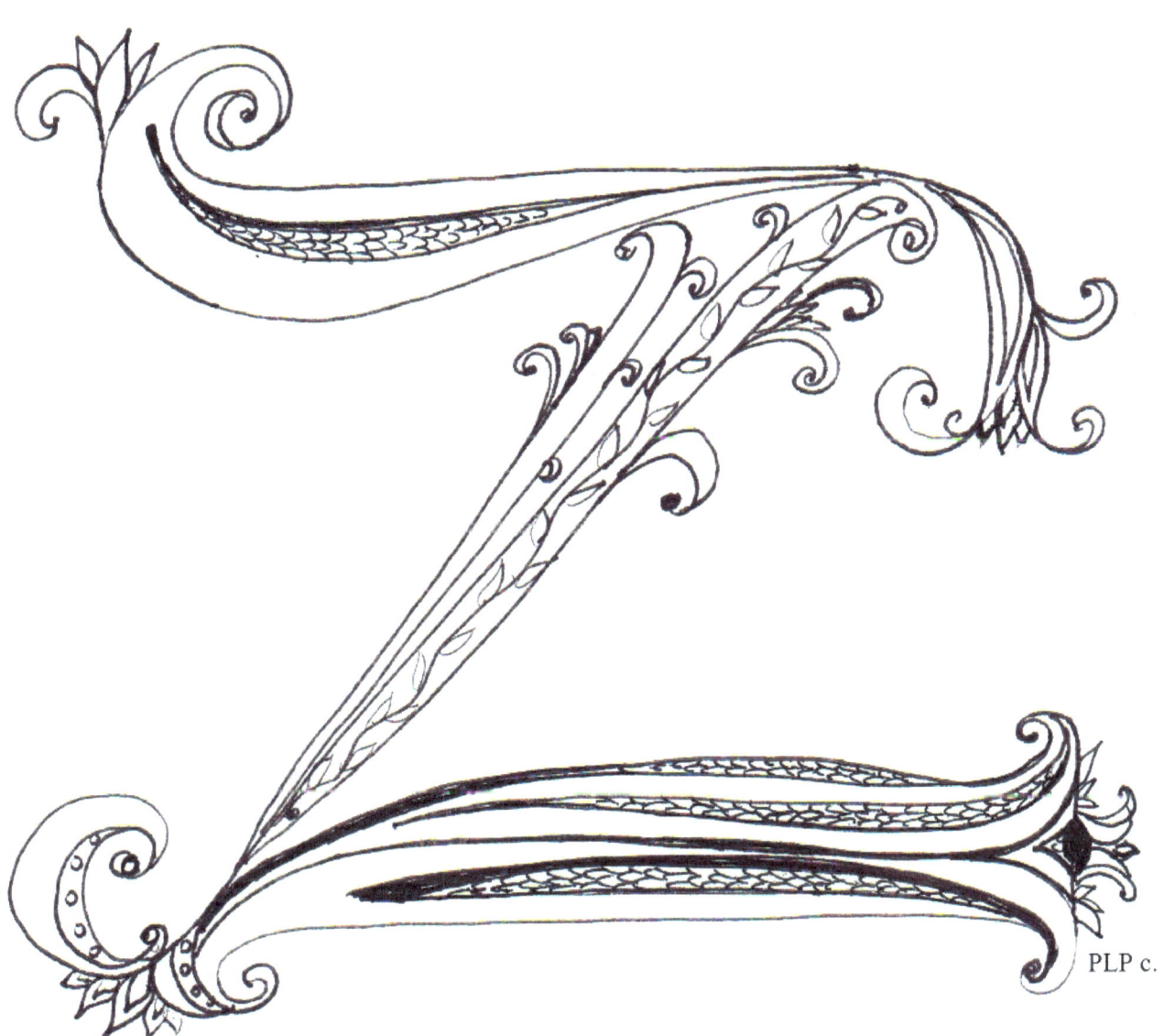

PLP c.

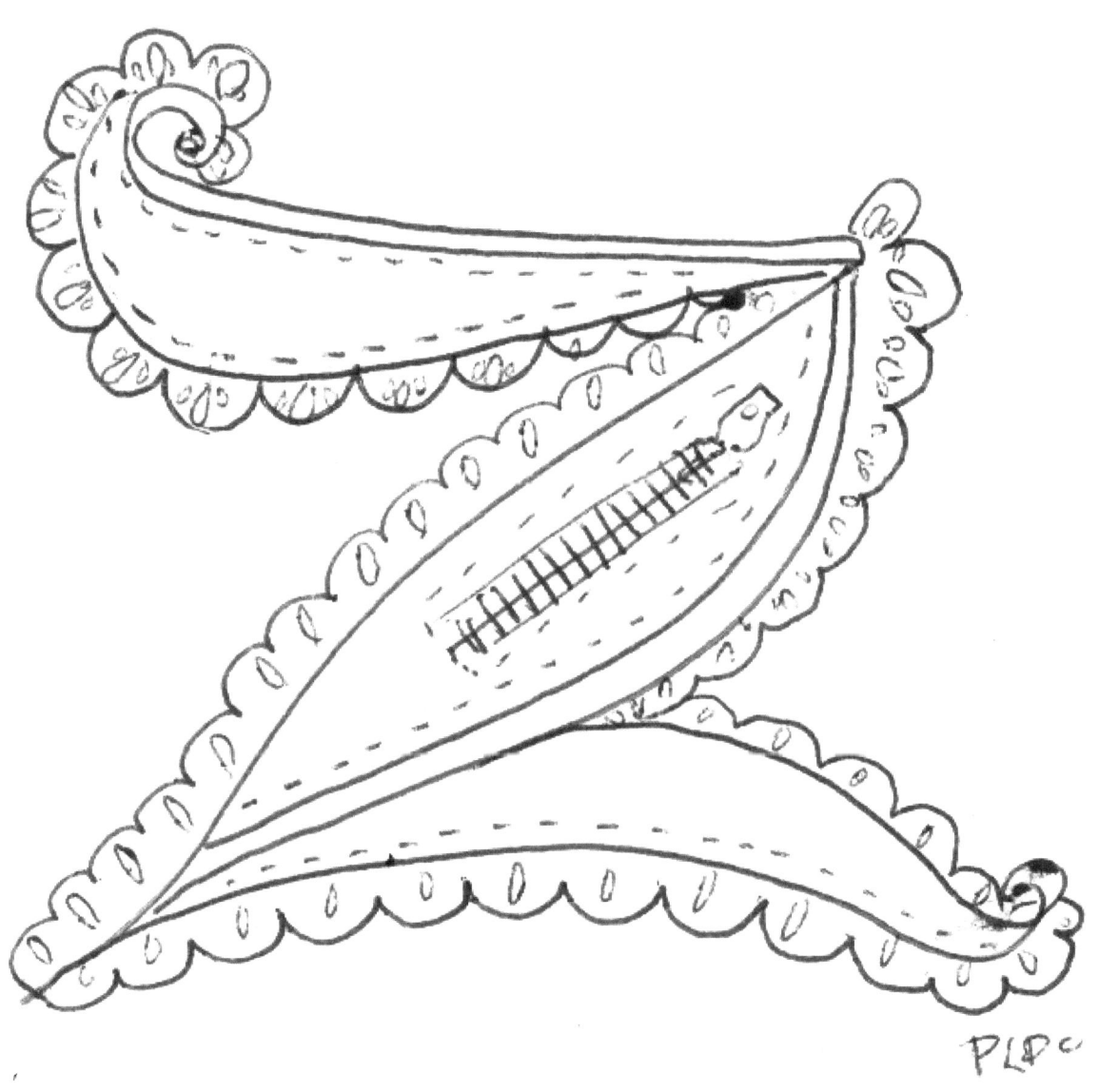

PHP

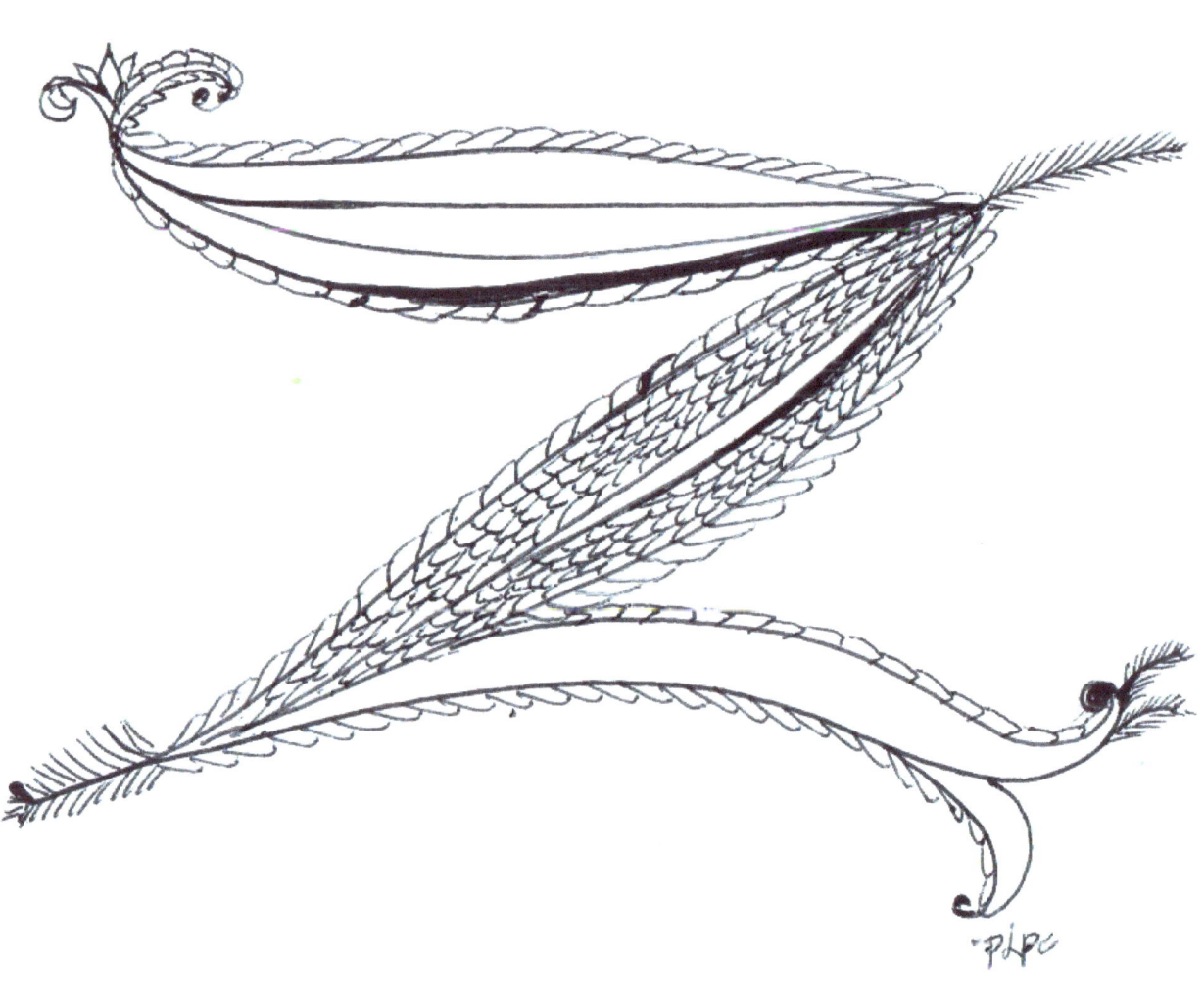

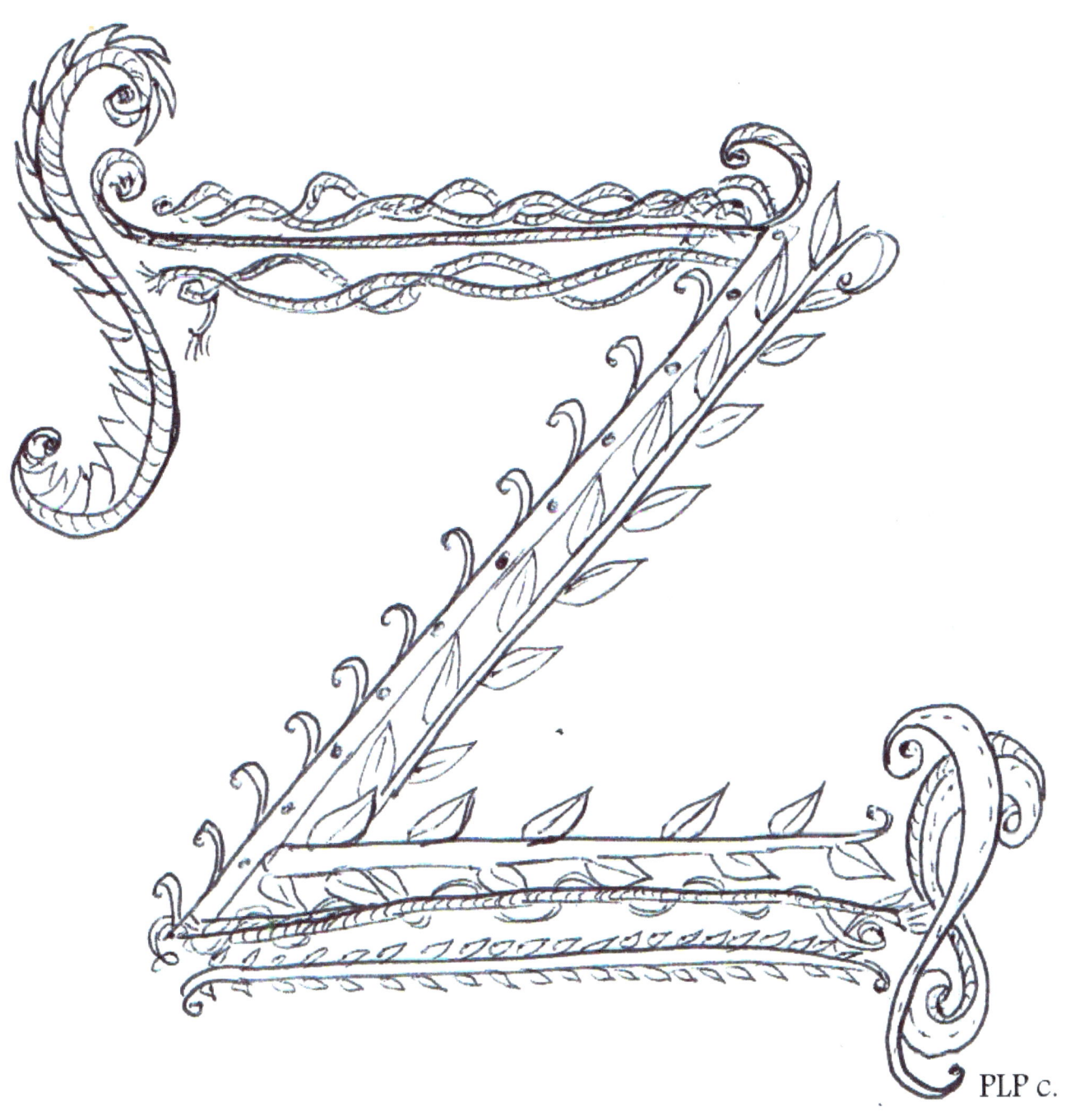

PLP c.

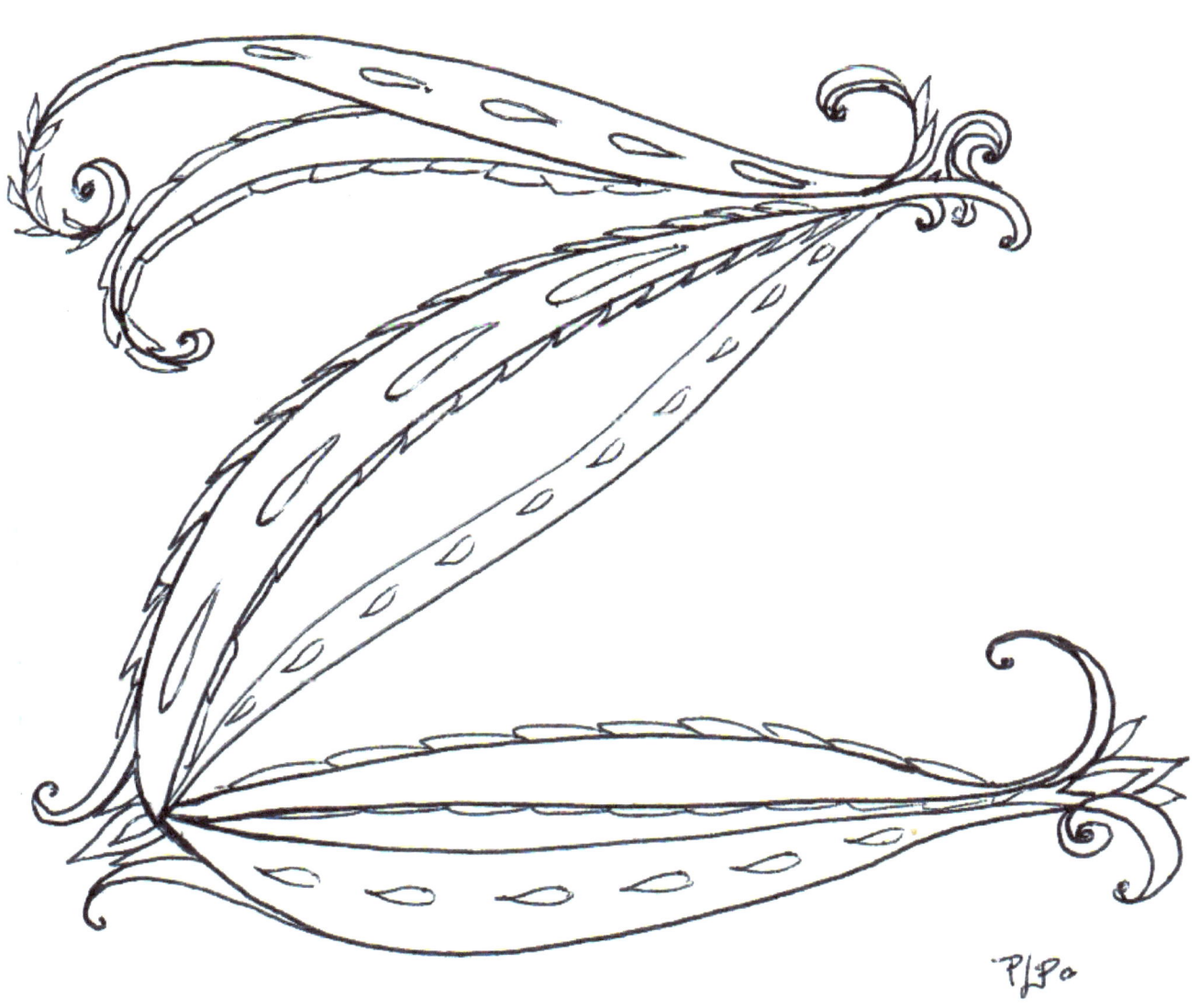

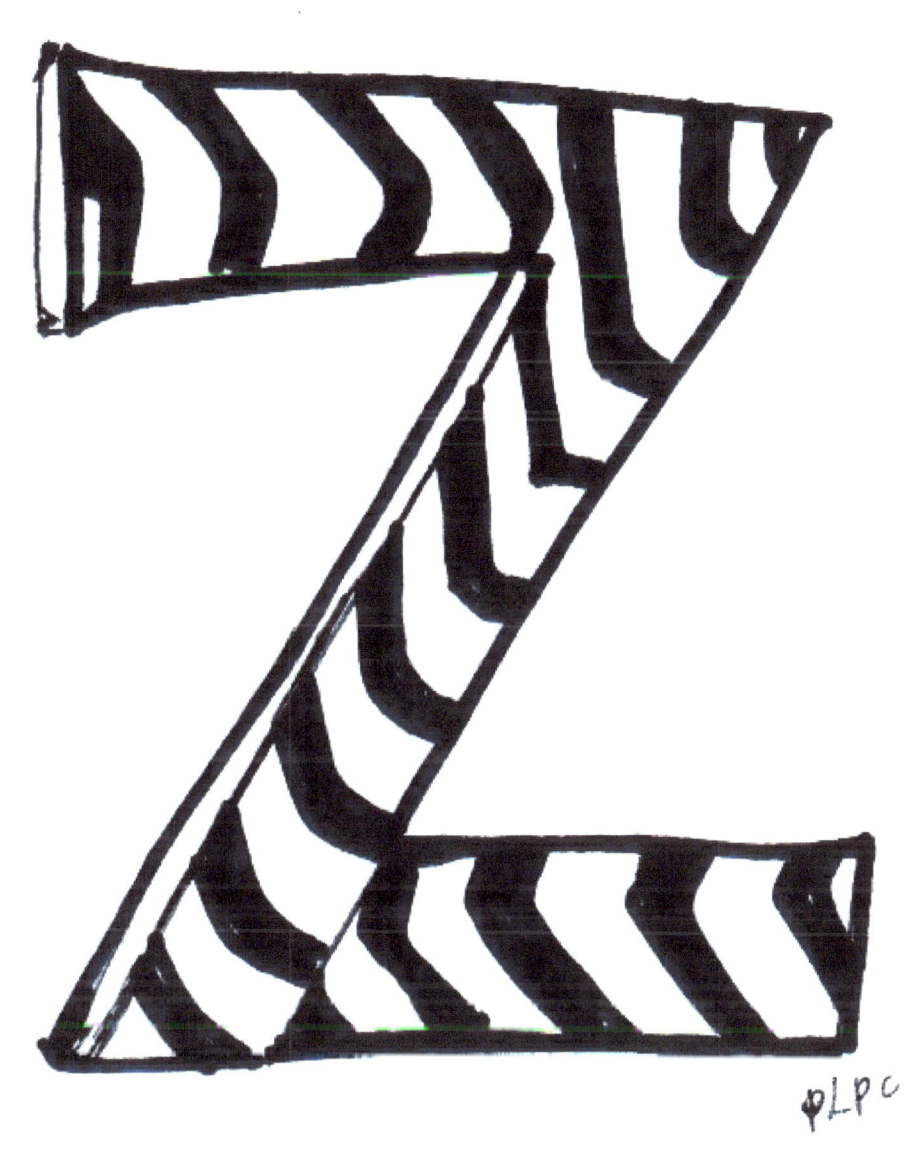

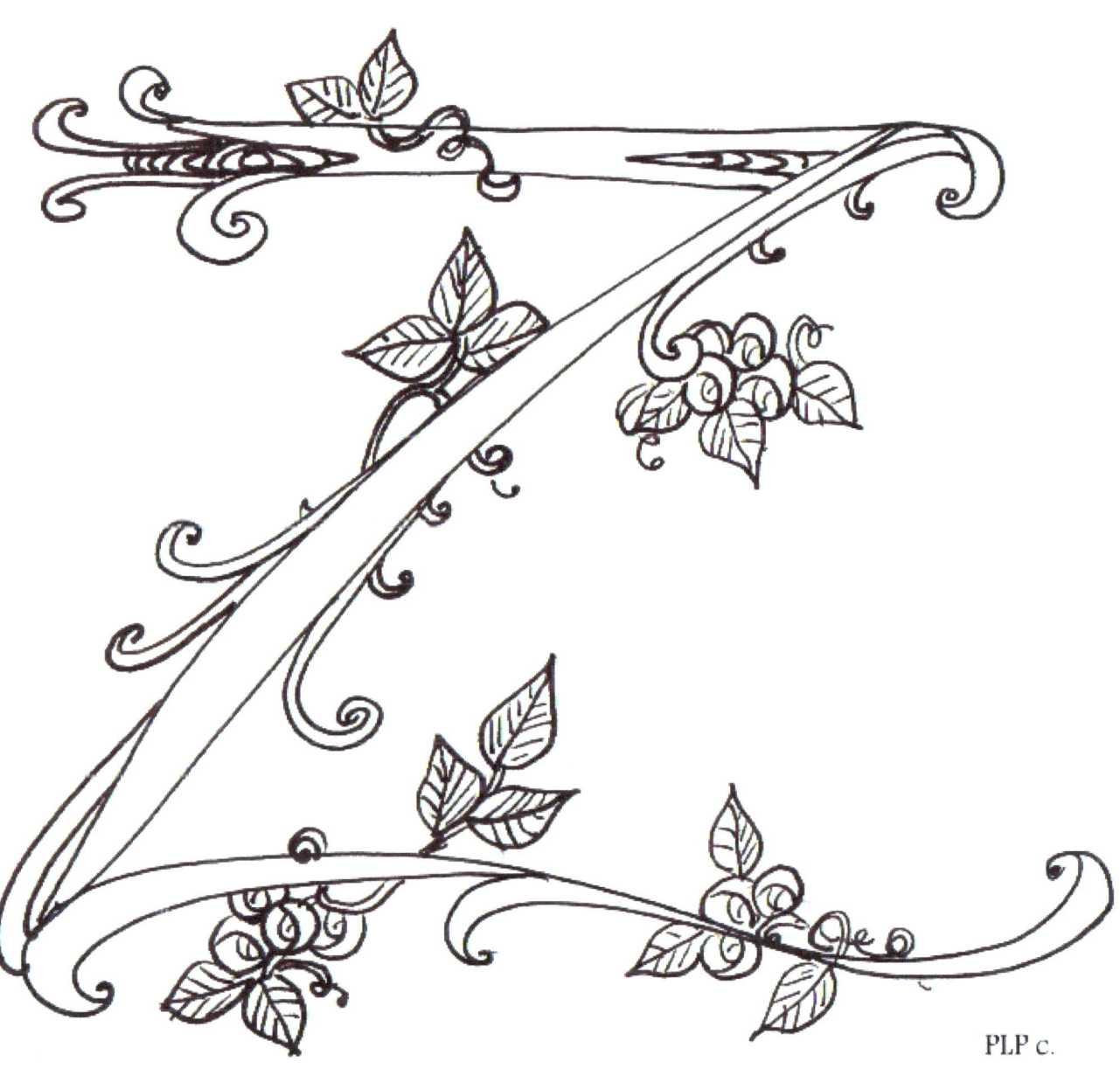

PLP c.

27

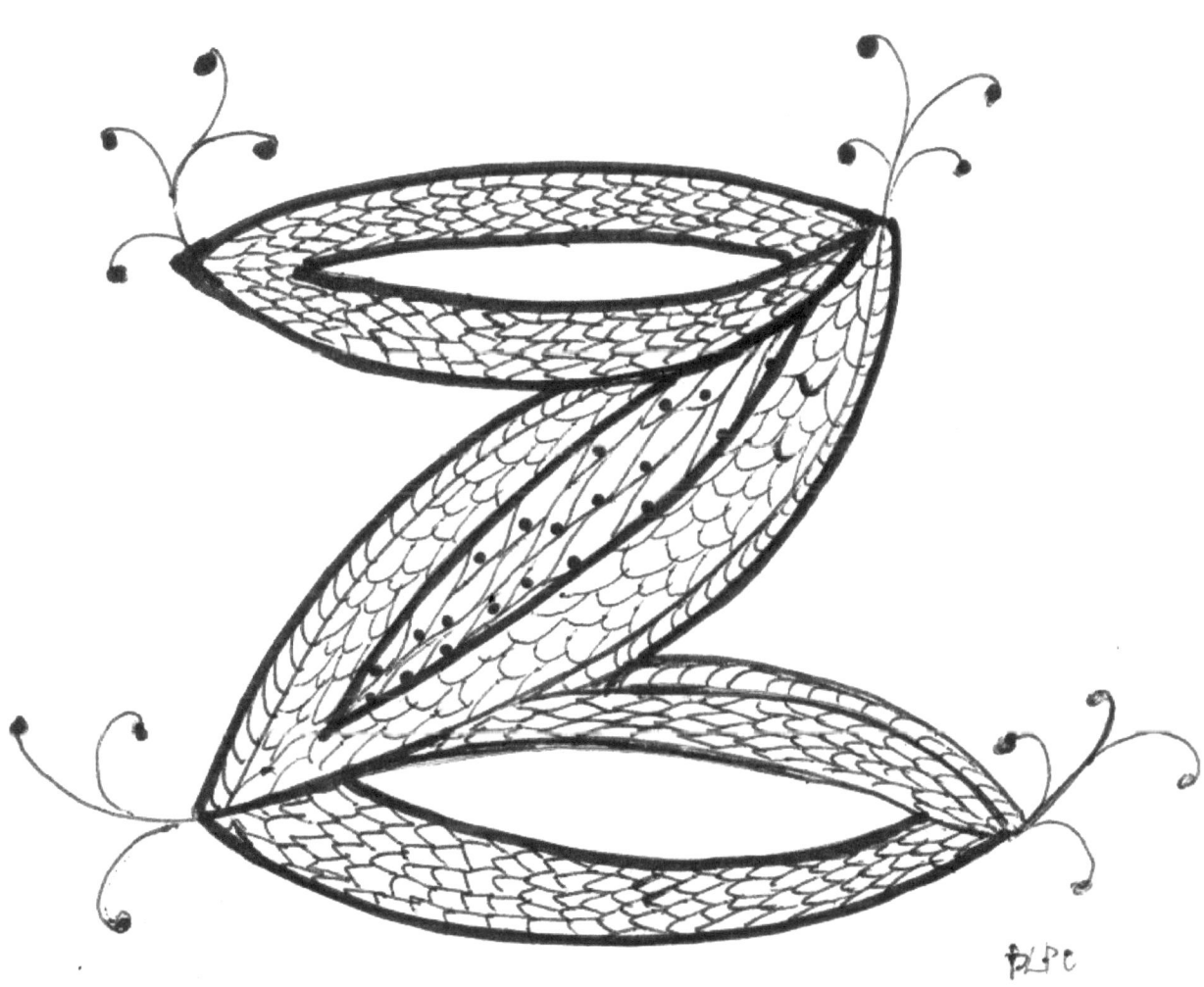

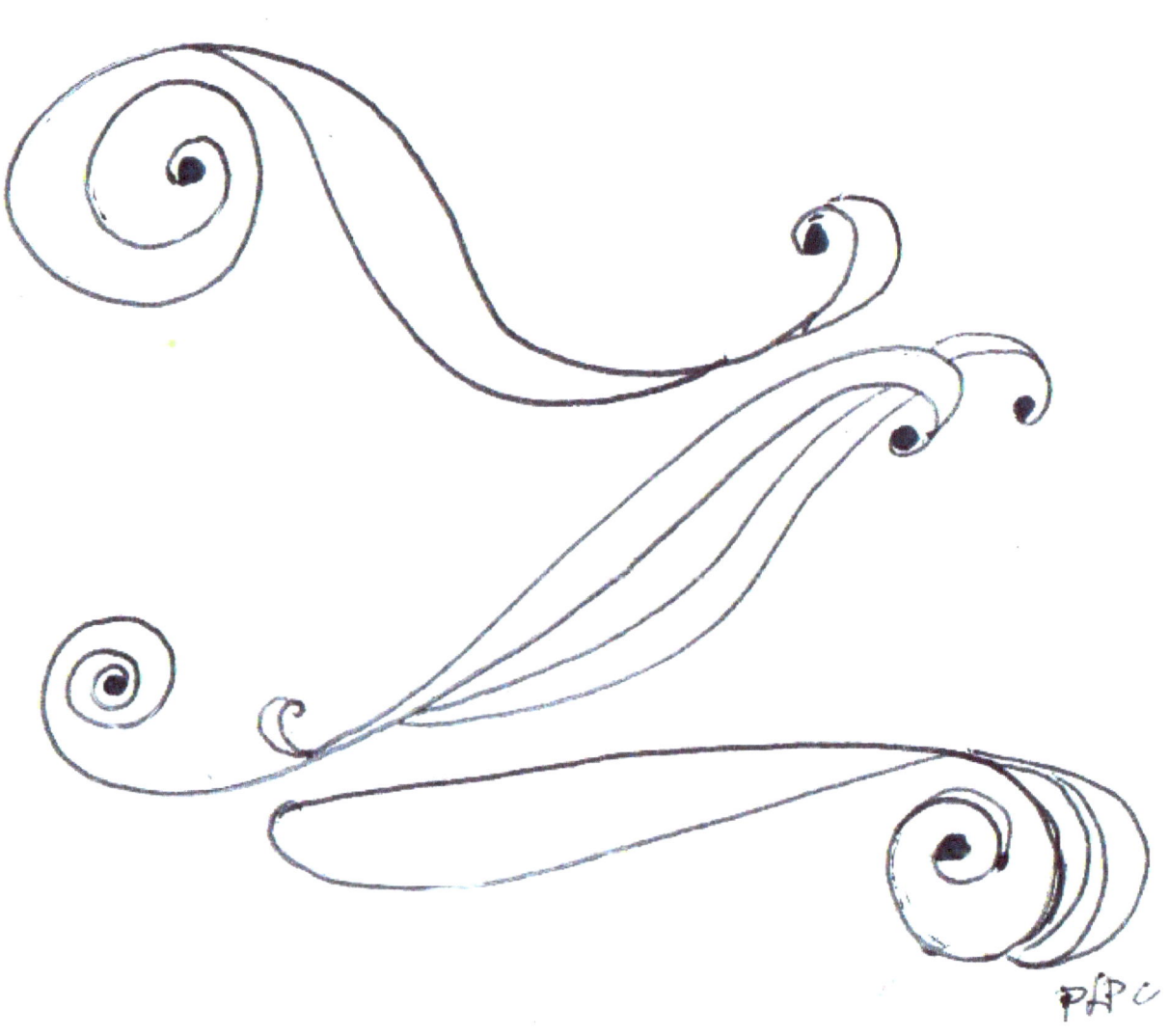

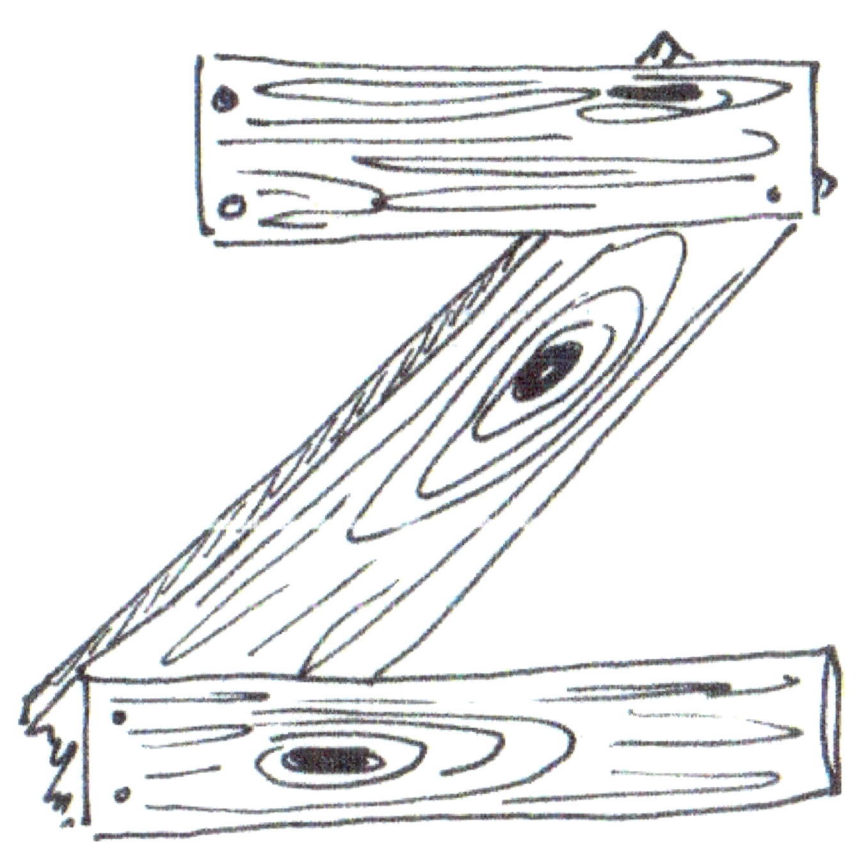

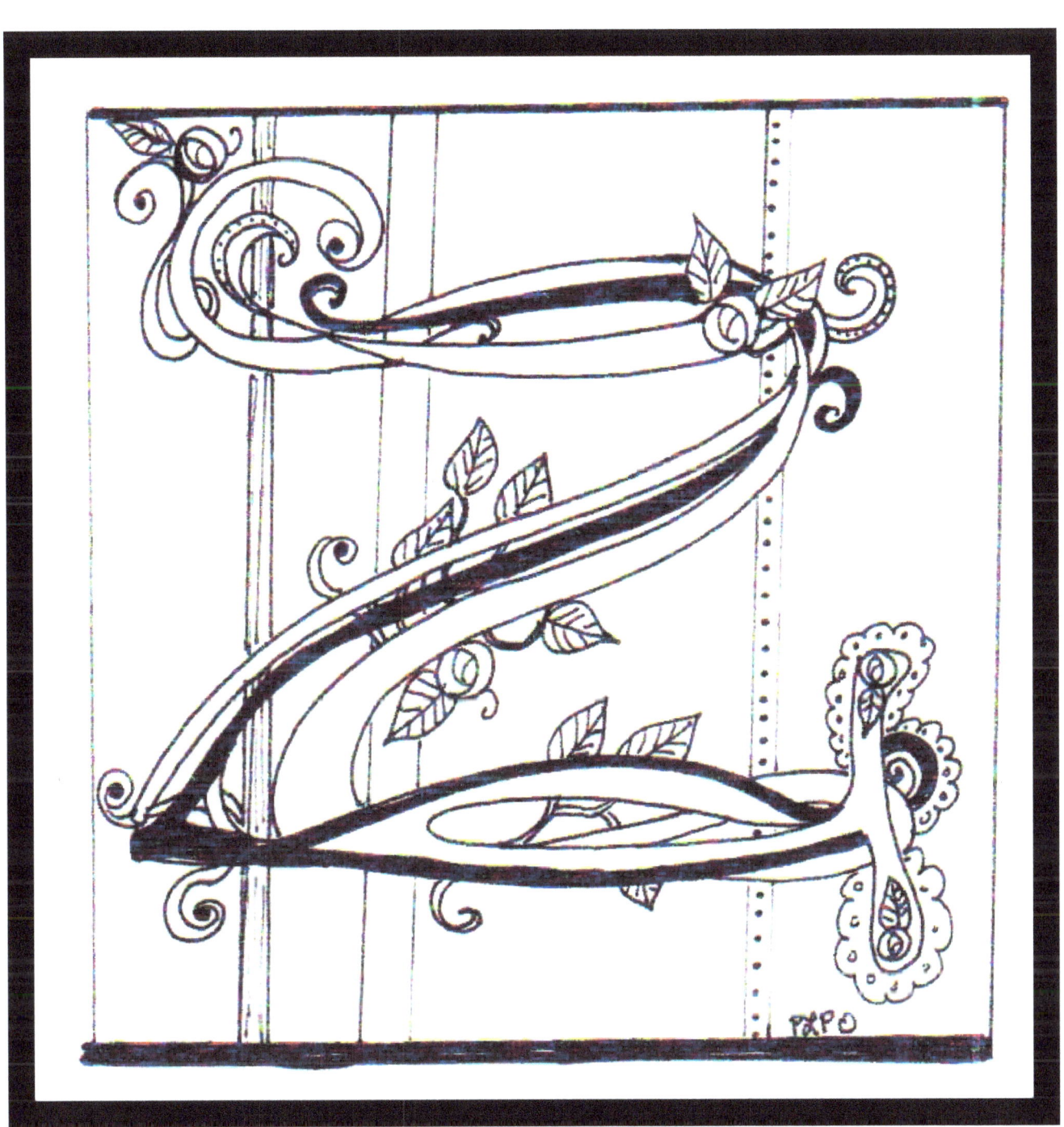

35

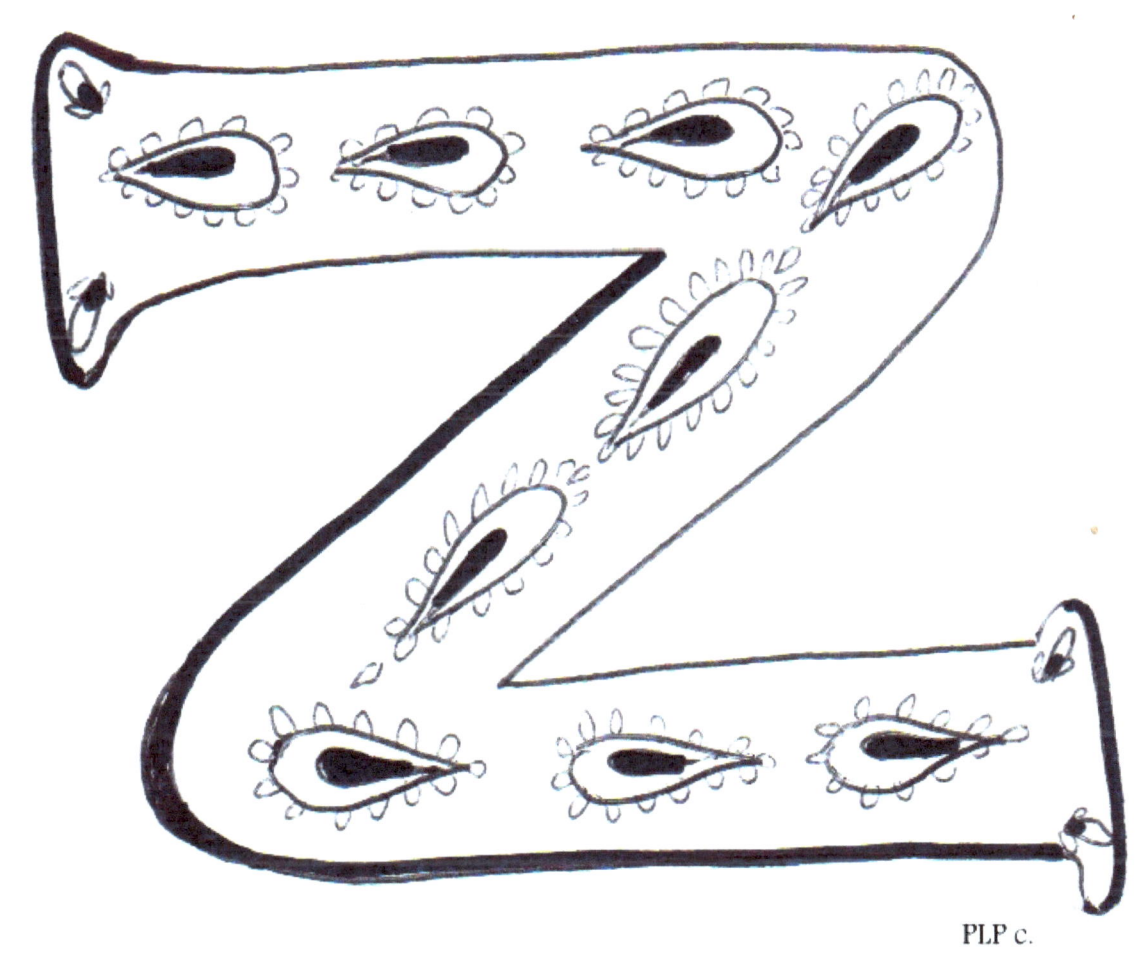

PLP c.

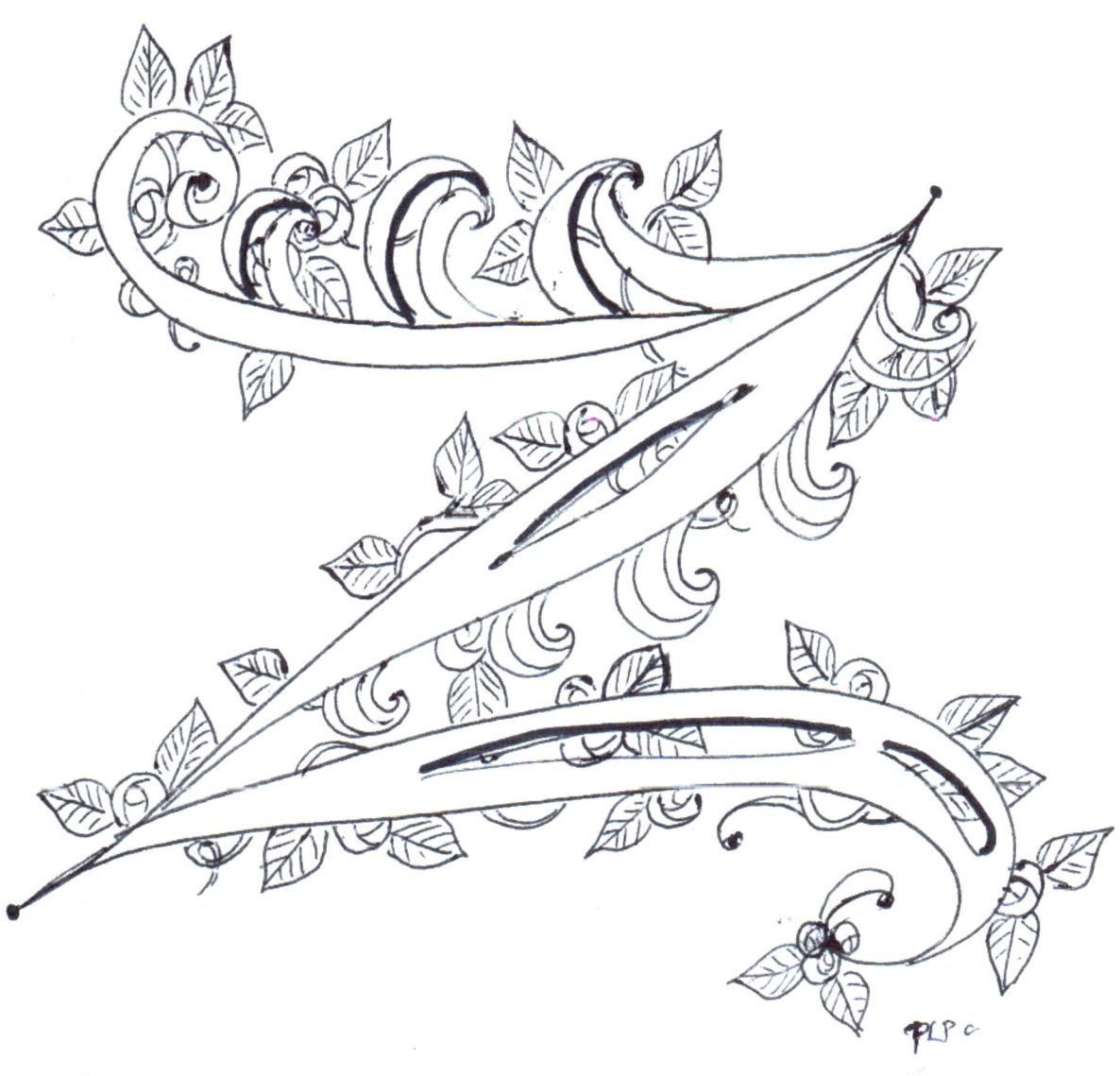

PLP c.

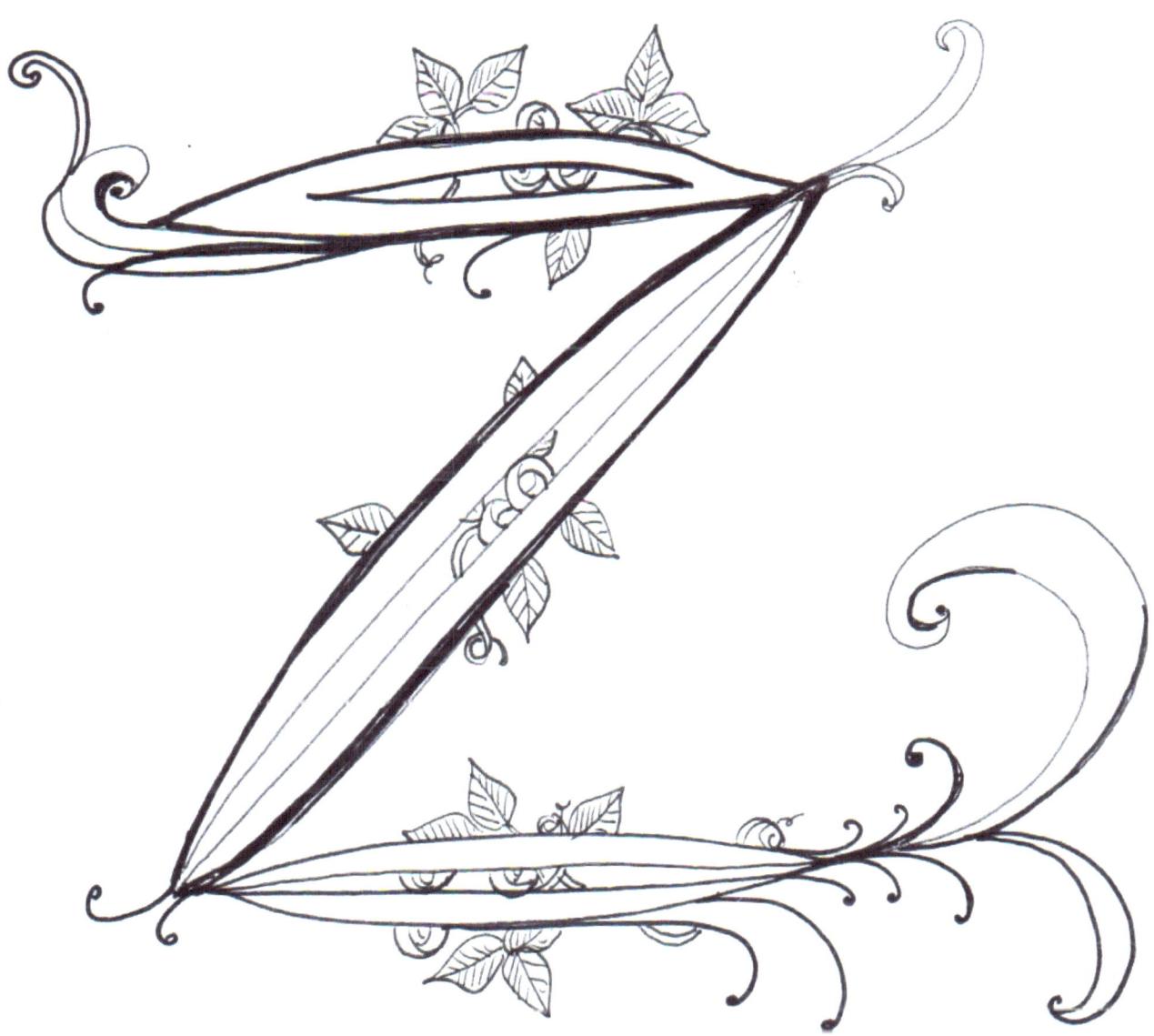

PLP c.

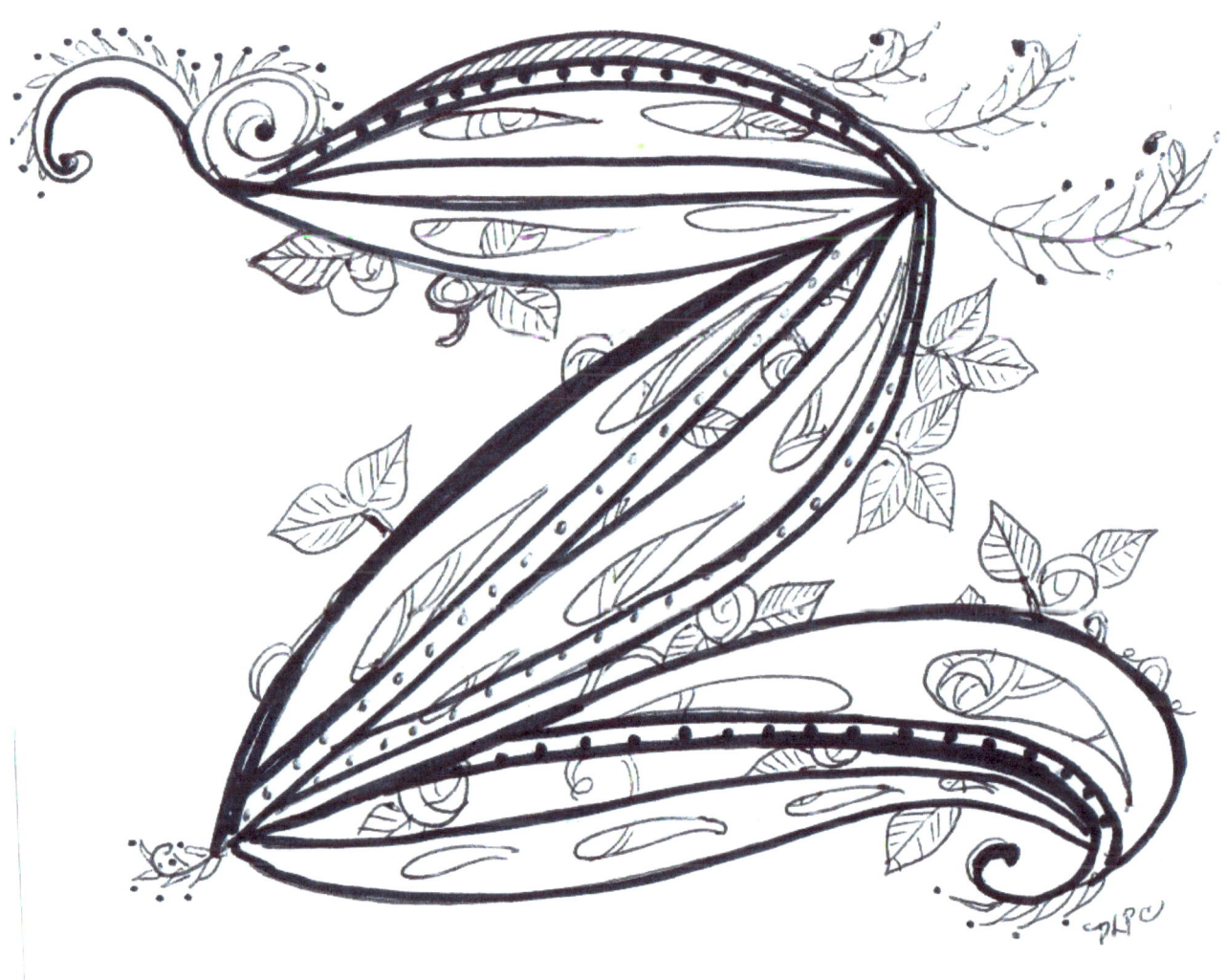

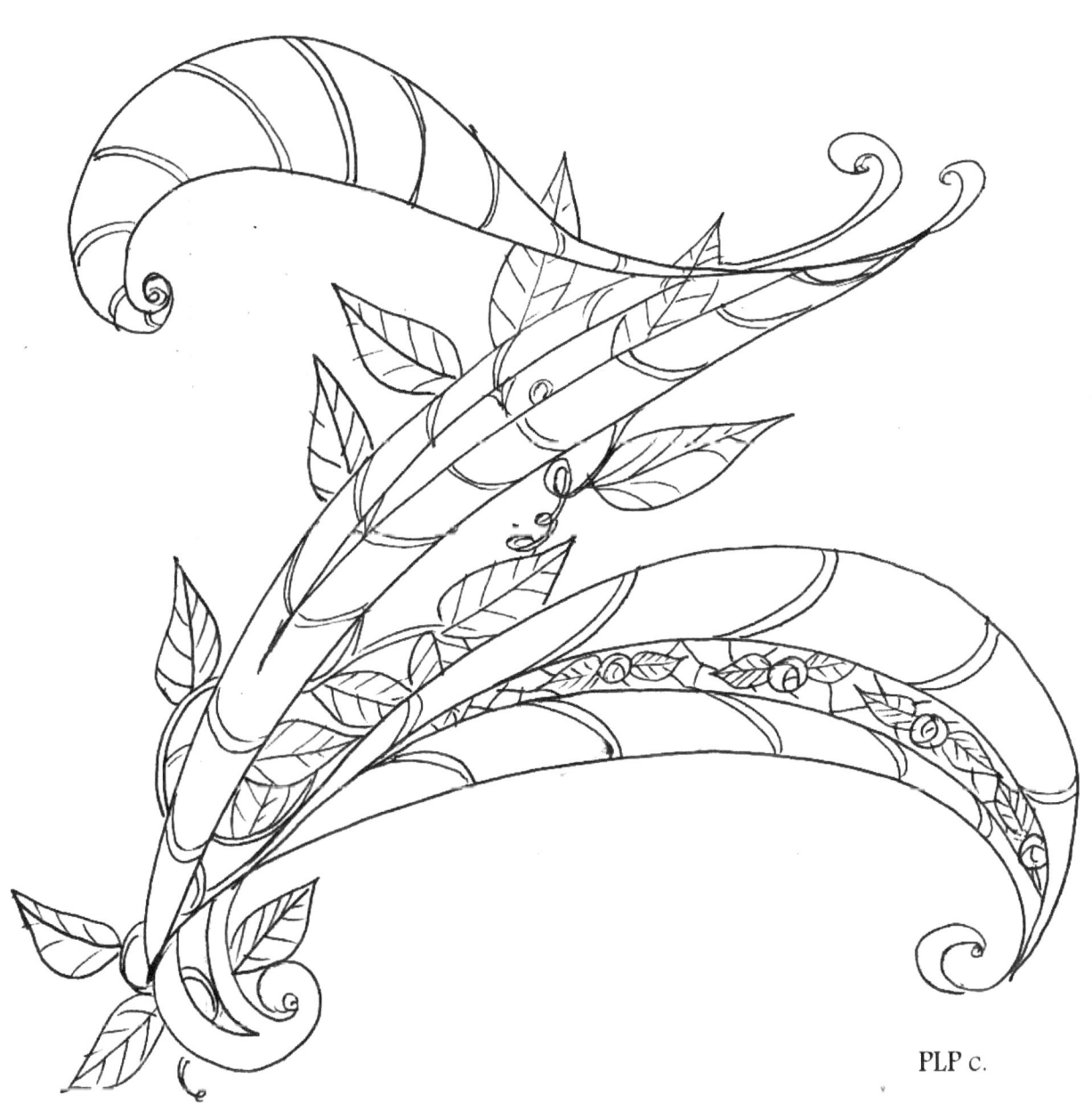

PLP c.

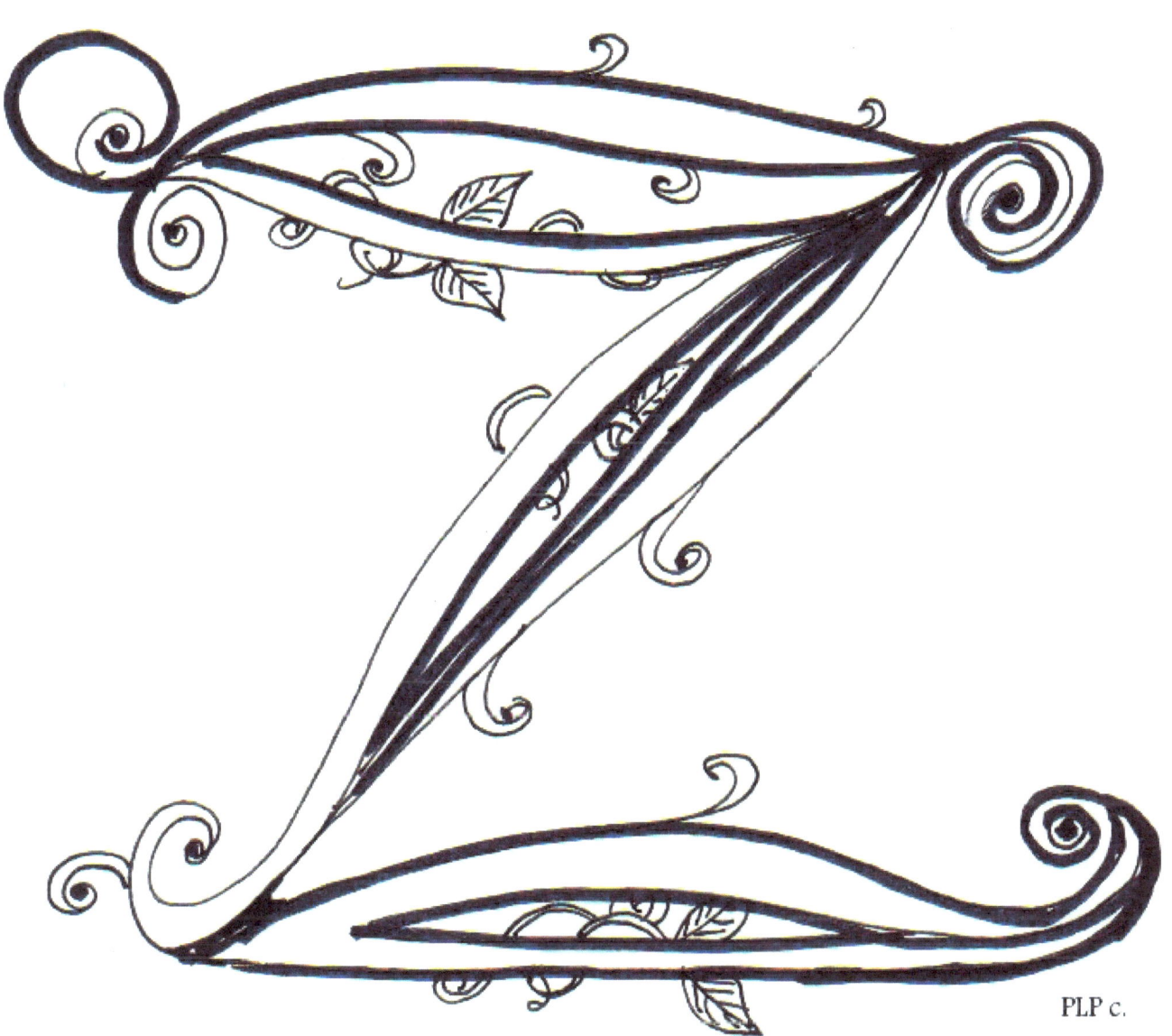

PLP c.

www.ingramcontent.com/pod-product-compliance
Lightning Source LLC
Chambersburg PA
CBHW051058180526
45172CB00002B/683